THE NEW HARTF
P.(
Central Aven
New Hartford, Connecticut 0600.
(860) 379-7235

D1055280

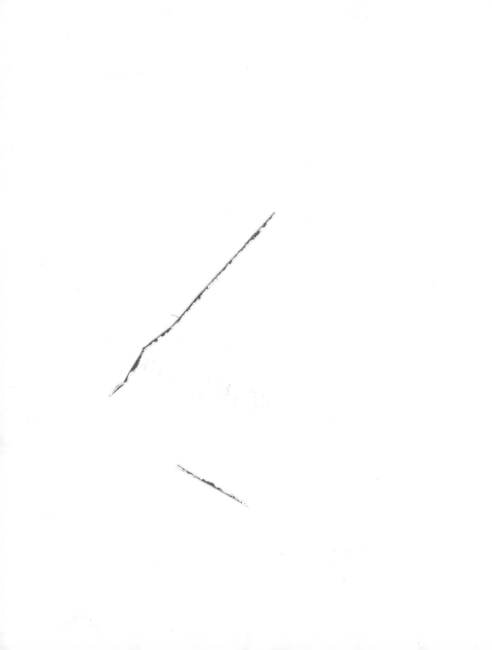

Rookie Read-About® Science

Solid, Liquid, or Gas?

By Fay Robinson

Consultants
Robert L. Hillerich, Professor Emeritus,
Bowling Green State University, Bowling Green, Ohio;
Consultant, Pinellas County Schools, Florida

Lynne Kepler, Educational Consultant

CHILDRENS PRESS®
CHICAGO

Design by Herman Adler Design Group
Photo Research by Feldman & Associates, Inc.

Library of Congress Cataloging-in-Publication Data

Robinson, Fay.
    Solid, liquid, or gas? / by Fay Robinson.
        p. cm. – (Rookie read-about science)
    Summary: Discusses the properties of solids, liquids, and gases,
the three forms in which matter exists.
    ISBN 0-516-06041-4
    1. Matter—Juvenile literature. [1. Matter.]
    I. Title. II. Series.
QC173.16.R63   1995
530.4–dc20   95-5563
                                                                CIP
                                                                AC

Look around. What do you
see and feel? The trees are
tall and bushy. The pond is
flat and still. The soft wind
feels warm on your face.

4

All of these things —
trees, water, and wind —
seem very different
from each other. But to
scientists, they all have
something important in
common. They are all
made of matter.

What is matter? Matter is anything that takes up space. That's just about everything!

Scientists sort all matter into three main groups — solids, liquids, and gases.

Solids all have their own shapes. What solids do you see around you? What shapes do they have?

A table, a chair, and a
book are all solids. So
are the wood and metal
they are made from.

You can't change the shape of a solid very easily — it always requires some work.

Water, juice, oil, and
milkshakes are liquids.
What shape is a milkshake?
If it is in a tall, thin glass,
it is tall and thin.

If it is in a wide, round
cup, it is wide and round.
So, while solids have their
own shape, liquids don't.

They take on the shape of
whatever container they are in.

Liquids can be poured from one container to another. Some liquids are thick and gooey. They pour slowly.

Some liquids are thin and
runny. They pour quickly.

Can you name a gas?

You might think of the gas at gas stations first. But the gas people put into cars is actually gasoline.

Gasoline is a liquid.

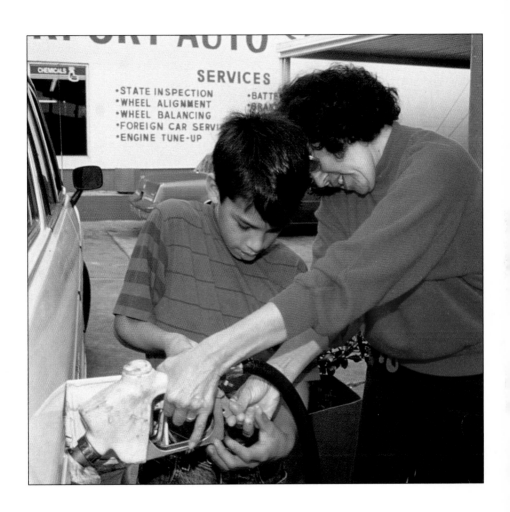

17

18

Most real gases are invisible. Air is gas. You can't see air, unless it is polluted and has smoke and other things in it.

The bubbles in a glass of soda are gas. This gas is called carbon dioxide and is one of the gases in air.

Helium is a gas that people sometimes use to fill balloons. Helium is lighter than air, so helium-filled balloons float.

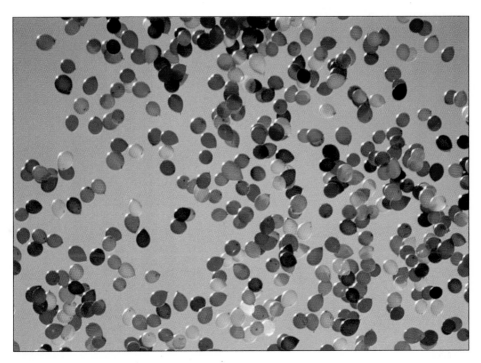

You can't pour a gas the way you can a liquid. Gas floats all around and spreads out.

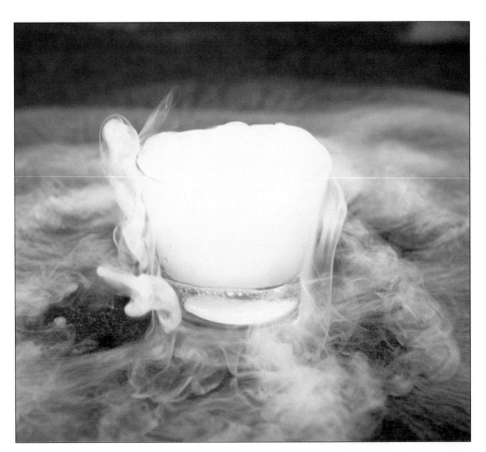

All matter, whether it is a solid, a liquid, or a gas, takes up space. It's easy to see that solids and liquids take up space.

But do gases take up space?

Blow up a balloon. You've just filled it with gases from your lungs.

The full balloon takes up a lot more space than an empty balloon because of the gas inside it.

Many things are a combination of solids, liquids, and gases. One of the best examples is you! Part of you is solid,

part of you is liquid,

and part of you is gas.

So no matter what
something looks like,
it's made of matter.

Look around again.
What solids, liquids,
and gases can you name?

Words You Know

matter

solids

wood table and chairs

books

rocks

trees

30

liquids

water

milkshake

gases

carbon dioxide bubbles

dry ice

31

Index

About the Author

Fay Robinson is an early childhood specialist who lives and works in the Chicago area. She received a bachelor's degree in Child Study from Tufts University and a master's degree in Education from Northwestern University. She has taught preschool and elementary children and is the author of several picture books.

Photo Credits

H. Armstrong Roberts – ©D. Logan, 4, 30 (bottom right)

Odyssey/Frerck/Chicago – ©Robert Frerck, 11

PhotoEdit – ©David Young-Wolff, 14

Photri – 25; ©Lani, 3

Root Resources – ©Gail Nachel, Cover

SuperStock International, Inc. – 20, 31 (bottom left); ©Dennis Junor, 7; ©Michael Rutherford, 13, 31 (top right); ©AGE Foto-Stock, 15, 31 (top left); ©Tom Rosenthal, 26, 27

Tony Stone Images – ©Paul McKelvey, 8, 30 (bottom left); ©Robert E. Daemmrich, 17; ©David Woodfall, 18

Unicorn Stock Photos – ©Joel Dexter, 21; Jim Shippee, 22, 31 (bottom right)

Valan – ©Jean Bruneau, 9, 30 (top left); ©Kennon Cooke, 28; ©V. Wilkinson, 30 (top right)

COVER: Balloon Fest